Rookie Read-About® Science

Stars in the Sky

By Allan Fowler

Consultants

Robert L. Hillerich, Professor Emeritus,
Bowling Green State University, Bowling Green, Ohio;
Consultant, Pinellas County Schools, Florida

Lynne Kepler, Educational Consultant

Fay Robinson, Child Development Specialist

Children's Press®
A Division of Grolier Publishing
New York   London   Hong Kong   Sydney
Danbury, Connecticut

Project Editor: Downing Publishing Services
Designer: Herman Adler Design Group
Photo Researcher: Feldman & Associates, Inc.

Library of Congress Cataloging-in-Publication Data

Fowler, Allan.
    Stars in the sky / by Allan Fowler.
        p. cm. – (Rookie read-about science)
    Includes index.
    Summary: A simple look at stars–what they are, where they are located,
how we see them.
        ISBN 0-516-06055-4
        1. Stars—Juvenile literature. [1. Stars.] I. Title. II. Series.
QB801.7.F79   1996
523.8—dc20
                                                    95-39677
                                                        CIP
                                                        AC

On a night when no clouds hide them from view, you can see hundreds of stars in the sky.

Some of those stars are bigger and hotter than our sun.

But because they are so far away, all stars look like tiny points of light.

5

All except one, the closest
star to us — our sun.

The earth is one of the sun's planets. A planet is a body that circles around a star.

A star shines by its
own light. Our daylight
is light from the sun.

The moon and planets do not shine by their own light. We can see them because the sun's light shines on them.

The nearest star beyond the sun is called Alpha Centauri. It is very far from us.

If we sent one of our
spaceships to Alpha
Centauri, it would take
hundreds and hundreds
of years to get there.

And most stars are much farther away than that.

Stars are not spread evenly in space.

They gather in groups called clusters.

13

14

Many clusters make
up a galaxy.

The galaxy we are
part of is known as
the Milky Way.

Can you imagine counting
every grain of sand on
a beach?

There could be that many
stars in just a single galaxy.

And there are that many
galaxies, or more, in space.
Nobody knows exactly
how many.

Not even astronomers —
people who study the
stars and other bodies
in space — know how
many stars there are.

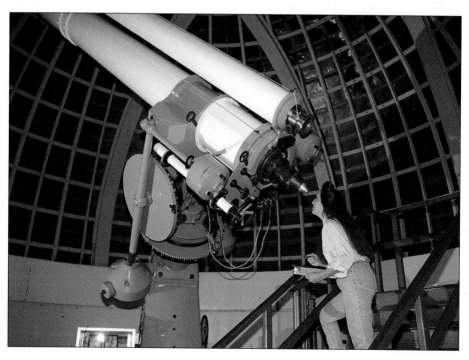

So on a clear, starry night,
you can see only a tiny,
tiny part of all the stars
there are.

Stars are huge balls of
a burning gas called
hydrogen. The hottest
stars are a bluish white.

Then, as they grow cooler,
they slowly change color —
to white . . . to yellow,
like our sun . . . and to red.

The stars help people
find their way around.
Long ago, travelers on

sea or land learned how
to tell where they were
by looking up at the stars.

Try it yourself!

On a clear night, look for seven stars that form the outline of a dipper or ladle.

The two stars on the outer edge of this Big Dipper's bowl point directly to a bright star called Polaris — the North Star.

Polaris is over the earth's North Pole. So if you face Polaris, you are facing north.

The streaks in this picture are called star trails. The bright mark in the middle is Polaris.

Do any stars, besides our sun, have planets circling them? Planets with life on them?

Many astronomers believe they do — but nobody knows for sure. Not yet.

What do *you* think?

Words You Know

moon

Planet Earth

star cluster

sun

stars

Milky Way galaxy

astronomer

Index

About the Author

Allan Fowler is a free-lance writer with a background in advertising. Born in New York, he lives in Chicago now and enjoys traveling.

Photo Credits

Tom Stack & Associates — ©Bill & Sally Fletcher, cover; ©Mike O'Brine, 13, 30 (bottom left)

Photo Edit — ©Tony Freeman, 3, 18, 31 (bottom right)

H. Armstrong Roberts — 20, ©ZEFA U.K./ZEFA, 5

Tony Stone Images, Inc. — ©Paul Fletcher, 6, 30 (bottom right); ©Lawrence Migdale, 29

Photri, Inc. — 7, 30 (top right); ©Lani Novak Howe, 17,

Valan Photos — ©Albert Kuhnigk, 8; ©Ian Davis-Young, 25

Dembinsky Photo Assoc. — ©Stan Osolinski, 9, 30 (top left); ©Pekka Parviainen, 27, 31 (top)

Visuals Unlimited — 10, 11, 14, 31 (bottom left)

Odyssey/Chicago — ©Joe Oliver, 19

Bettmann, 21, 22-23

COVER: Children looking at Milky Way